Navigating Blackboard

A Student's Guide
for Blackboard 6.0 and Blackboard 5.0

Hal Spiegel

Project Manager, eCampus Blackboard 5 System
LeCroy Center for Educational Telecommunication
Dallas County Community College District

PEARSON

Prentice
Hall

Upper Saddle River, New Jersey 07458

Acquisitions Editor: Alison Pendergast
Editor-in-Chief: Tracy Augustine
Director of Marketing: Jane Manning Hyatt
Development Editor: Carol Abalofia
Senior Managing Editor: Judy Leale
Design Manager: Maria Lange
Cover & Interior Design: Michael Fruhbeis
Associate Director, Multimedia Production: Karen Goldsmith
Manager, Print Production: Christy Mahon
Formatter: Carol O'Rourke
Manufacturing Buyer: Wanda Rockwell
Cover Printer: Phoenix Color, Inc.
Printer/Binder: Courier, Bookmart Press

Credits and acknowledgments borrowed from other sources and reproduced, with permission, in this textbook appear on appropriate page within text.

10 9 8 7 6 5 4 3
0-13-143151-X

Contents

Module 1 Introduction

What Is Blackboard?

Blackboard is a comprehensive e-Learning software platform that delivers a course management system through the flexibility of the Internet. This system offers you a set of robust tools, functions, and features for interactive learning. Professors are able to customize content based on the your needs and course requirements. Using the system's many features, you are able to read announcements, access assignments, take tests, upload completed projects, and communicate with the instructor and other students.

Learning with a Course Management System

You may be new to using an online course management system, or perhaps you have had experience with one before. In either case, here is a checklist to help you become a better learner in an online environment.

✔ **Take time to familiarize yourself with the Web site for your course**. Find out the course schedule, the course requirements, the method for contacting your instructor, the help files, and so on.

✔ **Review any informational files on your course, and experiment with the navigation.** Try the different links to see where they go. (No, you won't destroy anything by doing this!)

✔ **Log in to the course site regularly**. Look for announcements or updates to the course.

✔ **Participate in the activities that have been designed for your course—bulletin board discussions, chat sessions, and so on**. These activities are part of your classroom experience.

✔ **Contact your instructor (or whomever your instructor has appointed) whenever you have questions or problems with the software**. You can also post questions to your class discussion area. Your classmates may answer you before your instructor does.

✔ **Plan for deadlines**. Computers are much less forgiving than your instructor! If a test needs to be taken by 4 P.M., Blackboard will not allow you to access it at 4:01.

✔ **Be prepared**. Keep in mind that your Internet connectivity may have disruptions in service. It is possible that your or your school's Internet service may become unavailable. It is a good idea to leave a little extra time for connecting, uploading, and downloading files to ensure you meet your deadlines.

✔ **Remember that your online course is a public place**. Speak and behave with the same politeness and respect expected in any classroom. (If you find you've posted something that embarrasses you or that gives the wrong impression, ask your instructor to remove it from the course site.)

For further information about learning effectively with Blackboard, consult: **http://www.blackboard.com**.

Tips for Becoming a Successful Online Learner

Congratulations! You are about to embark on a journey that will take your learning to a new level. You may meet some new challenges along the way. This guide will help you meet those challenges by helping you begin to navigate Blackboard to find many online resources intended to help you succeed in the course you are studying. You're on your way to becoming a successful online learner.

COMMUNICATION

✔ Know how to access your Blackboard course Web site along with your login information. Ask your instructor.

✔ Check the site frequently for changes and updates.

✔ Learn and use proper "netiquette" by visiting Web sites such as the St. Louis Community College guide at
http://www.stlcc.cc.mo.us/distance/text/netiquette.html.

ORGANIZATION AND TIME MANAGEMENT

✔ Develop a system to keep track of assignments, deadlines, and materials.

✔ Schedule time on a regular basis to review your assignments and activities and to back-up and save your work.

✔ Be realistic by setting interim goals and deadlines for yourself and stick to them!

✔ Attend a time management seminar or learn about time management on the Web at a site like Harper College's PowerPoint presentation at
http://www.harpercollege.edu/doit/dlinfo/tmpres.shtml.

MOTIVATION

✔ Stick to your time-management plan and schedules by staying motivated.

✔ Some motivation tips from University of Texas Austin can be found at
http://www.utexas.edu/student/utlc/makinggrade/practical.html.

ACTIVE LEARNING

✔ Become an active learner by determining your personal learning style and taking advantage of how you learn best.

✔ You can discover your learning style by taking an assessment such as the DVC Survey by Catherine Jester on the Internet at **http://www.metamath.com/multiple/multiple_choice_questions.cgi.**

CRITICAL THINKING

✔ Just because it's on the Internet, don't believe that everything you read is true.

✔ Learn to evaluate sources.

✔ University of Minnesota's Web site provides a starting point for you to discover the benefits of critical thinking at **http://www.extension.umn.edu/distribution/citizenship/DH5645.html.**

EFFECTIVE READING

✔ Be sure to read your instructor's directions and assignments carefully.

✔ Take advantage of reading resources to get the most out of your Pearson textbook and the course's Blackboard Web site by learning more about reading effectively.

✔ Visit the Dartmouth College Web site at

http://www.dartmouth.edu/%7eacskills/success/reading.html for more information on reading.

TECHNOLOGY

✔ Plan ahead for technical glitches because they will happen. Sometimes access is unavailable or a computer lab may be full.

✔ Allow extra time for completing coursework so that technical glitches don't cause you to miss a deadline.

✔ Learn how to use your school's version of Blackboard and know the course policies, so that you can focus on the course content.

CAMPUS RESOURCES

✔ Your school will probably have some type of support services for Blackboard. Take advantage of these services, which may include help services, tutorials, or booklets written just for your school.

✔ Most schools have an academic support or study-skills office that is ready to help you adapt to the online learning environment. Visit their office or Web site.

✔ Some schools provide support online for Blackboard on the campus Web site. Find out if your school provides additional support online

✔ Ask your classmates for help too. They may have an idea or solution they can share with you.

Stay focused and have fun!

Module 2 Getting Started with Blackboard

Basic Computer Requirements

Following are the minimum hardware requirements:

✔ 75Mhz Pentium or equivalent
✔ 32 Megabytes of RAM
✔ 14.4 modem with Internet access
✔ preferred—multimedia capabilities with sound and CD-ROM

We recommend that you get the fastest multimedia computer and modem that you can, with as much RAM as possible. The faster your system, the less time you will spend waiting. If you are using the latest browsers, their minimum requirements are a Pentium III with 128MB of RAM. Let your budget be your guide.

Internet Access

You can access your college or university Blackboard system from anywhere you find an Internet connection. Access speed will vary depending on your data connection. For example, a campus lab may offer a T1 connection rate that transfers information at 1.5 MB per second, while your home computer may have a rate of 28 KB per second. This would mean that you could access information more than 50 times faster on campus than at home. Speed will vary depending on the number of simultaneous users.

Choosing a Browser

Blackboard functions the same across both Apple and PC based platforms. No matter which computer system you use, it must run Netscape 4.0 (or higher) or Internet Explorer 4.0 (or higher) as your Internet browser in order to access Blackboard. Blackboard has suggested versions of browsers that have been thoroughly tested and are recommended for using this system. See Figure 8.4 on page 56 in the "Frequently Asked Questions" section for these suggestions.

Browser Settings

Blackboard uses the full potential of the Internet's capabilities, and in order for your setup to work correctly, you must set your browser to accept all cookies and have Java and JavaScript enabled. These options are set correctly when your browser is initially installed using the default settings. Changing these options may be necessary only if you are using someone else's computer like a friend's or the campus lab's where these options may have been modified. It is always good to check with the lab technician or the owner of the computer before making any of these modifications. This example uses Netscape 7.0 on a Windows XP platform. If you need additional assistance, refer to Help in the menu bar of your browser.

NETSCAPE SETUP

First open your Netscape Browser. Click on **Edit**, then **Preferences**. (See Figure 2.1.)

After you click **Preferences**, the preferences box appears. In the lower left-hand area, click the **Advanced** option. Your right-hand panel options will change from the Navigator option to the Advanced

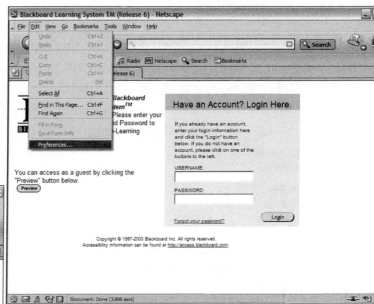

FIGURE 2.1 NETSCAPE SETUP.
You will find Preferences under the Edit menu option.

option. If there is not a check there already, place a check to the left of these items: Enable Java, XSLT, Enable Quick Launch. (See Figure 2.2.)

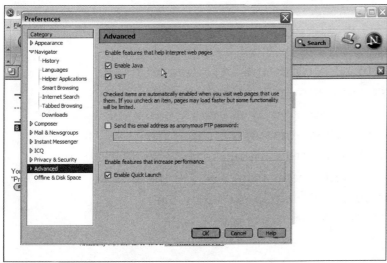

FIGURE 2.2 ADVANCED OPTIONS.
After highlighting **Advanced**, you can enable Java. This example uses Netscape 7.0 on a Windows XP platform. If you need additional assistance, refer to Help in the menu bar of your browser.

Next, click in **Scripts & Plugins**. At the top you will see: Enable JavaScript for—**Navigator** needs to be checked. At the bottom, checks need to be placed by both: Create or change cookies and Read cookies. (See Figure 2.3.) Additional options that are checked will not affect the functionality of Blackboard. Click **OK** once you've made these selections.

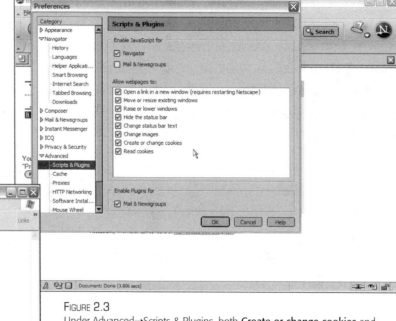

FIGURE 2.3
Under Advanced→Scripts & Plugins, both **Create or change cookies** and **Read cookies** need to be enabled.

INTERNET EXPLORER SETUP

The setup for Microsoft's Internet Explorer is a little different. First, open Internet Explorer, then click on **Tools** and **Internet Options**, as Figure 2.4 shows.

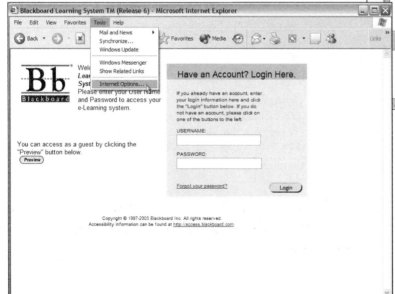

FIGURE 2.4 INTERNET EXPLORER SETUP.
You will find Internet Options under the Tools menu.

Next, click on **Security**. (See Figure 2.5.) At the bottom of the box that appears you will see a button that reads Default Level. By clicking this option you will reset your Internet Explorer to its original security settings, which meet Blackboard's needs. Next, click the **Advanced** tab in the top right-hand corner. At the bottom of the box you

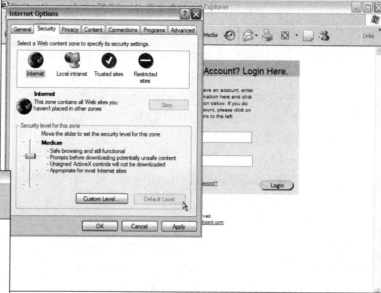

FIGURE 2.5 INTERNET EXPLORER AND BLACKBOARD.
You will find the Default Level button under the Security tab.

will see Restore Defaults. Click this to restore the original settings. See Figure 2.6 if you have any questions.

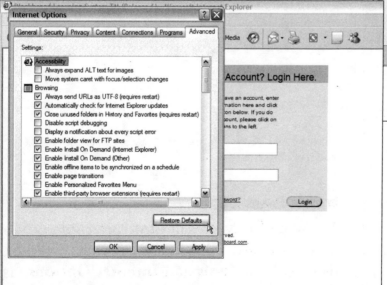

FIGURE 2.6 INTERNET EXPLORER AND RESTORE DEFAULTS.
You will find the Restore Defaults button under the Advanced tab.

Special Plugins

Courses may require plugins that allow specific types of content to play on your computer, like video segments, PowerPoint presentations, and Flash animations. Ask your instructor if your course requires any specific plugins.

Module 3 Accessing Blackboard

To access your institution's Blackboard Web site, you must have the Web address, often called its URL (Universal Resource Locator). The college catalog and the campus' Web site usually provide links to this site, but if you cannot find this information, contact your professor. Your professor is usually the best resource for answers to your questions.

Bookmarks and Blackboard

Bookmarks are not functional within Blackboard because Blackboard uses dynamically created Web pages. For example, imagine you were in a document within a specific area of your course, like the course syllabus, and you created a bookmark with the idea of being able to easily return to the syllabus later. Your bookmark would not work once you logged out of that session. If you later tried to use your bookmark, you would first be taken to a login screen and then brought to a general area within your course.

Logging into Blackboard

After you have the URL for your school's Blackboard system, enter it into the address bar of your browser. There are two different views that may appear depending on how your college or university chose to set up Blackboard. Figure 3.1 demonstrates the standard login screen, and Figure 3.2 shows direct portal entry. The main benefit to direct portal entry is that the student is not required to log in to receive information. Campus news, login procedures, and other vital information can be presented without anyone logging in. Figure 3.2 is an example of the Dallas County Community College District's direct portal entry page. This view is customized and information is updated on a daily basis to better serve the students and faculty.

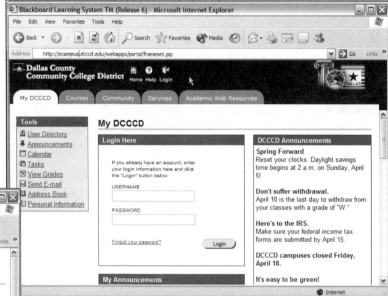

FIGURE 3.2 AN EXAMPLE OF DIRECT PORTAL ENTRY.
Without logging in, students can receive vital information about their campus.

If your campus uses direct portal entry, you can get to the same login screen by clicking the login option at the top of the screen. (See Figure 3.2.)

After you click the Login button on the Blackboard homepage, you will be prompted for your

FIGURE 3.1 BLACKBOARD LOGIN SCREEN.
Your login screen may look different.

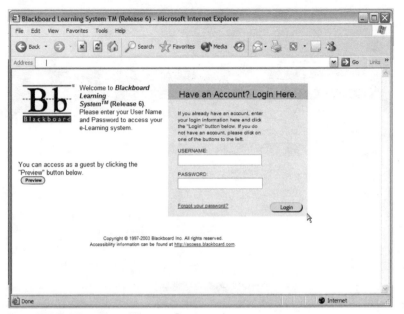

FIGURE 3.3 THE BLACKBOARD WELCOME SCREEN.
After you enter your username and password, click the **Login** button.

username and password (see Figure 3.3). The login and password that you use allows Blackboard to recognize you as a unique person within the system. When you take a test, submit a document, or answer a discussion question, Blackboard attaches your identification to the transaction. Any time you do anything on the system, your actions are tracked. Keep your username and password secure; do not give them to anyone.

If you forget your password, click the **Forgot your password**? option. If your campus is using direct portal entry, you will need to click **Login** at the top of the screen to see this option. An e-mail will be sent to you with a URL that will grant you temporary access and allow you to reset your password under the Personal Information option. Blackboard's ability to help you when you forget your password is one of the main reasons that you should add your e-mail address to the system after you first log in. We will discuss changing your password in Personal Information in Module 4.

Enter your username and password, then click **Login**. If you do not know your username and password, contact the instructor or the registrar's office. *Note*: Your username will always stay the same in the system, but you, your instructor, or the system administrator may change your password.

Blackboard User Interface

Once you have clicked **Login**, the Blackboard user interface appears. The Blackboard E-Learning System is a one-login/one-user entry methodology. This means that when you log into the system, it recognizes you through your login. In Figure 3.4, it states Welcome John. By logging in, only the information that is relevant to you appears on your screen.

Navigating Blackboard

Blackboard has navigation built into the system. The tabs you see across the top in Figure 3.4—My Institution, Courses, Community, Services, and Academic Web Resources—are one way to move

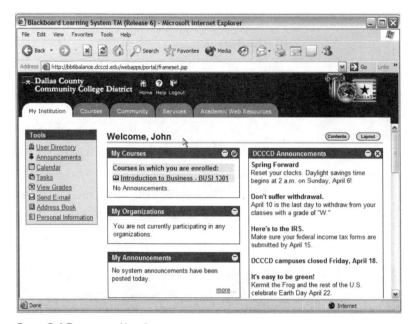

FIGURE 3.4 BLACKBOARD USER INTERFACE.

among different areas within the Blackboard system. The navigation located on the left-hand side of the screen allows for navigation within specific areas. For example, Tools navigation appears under the My Institution tab.

It's important to note that your college or university can rename the tabs that appear in Blackboard. For example, in Figure 3.4 you will see the My Institution tab, however in Figure 3.5 the same tab is named My DCCCD. The naming of the My DCCCD tab has been customized to reflect the college it represents. My DCCCD stands for My Dallas County Community College District.

Another way to move around in Blackboard is with the "breadcrumb trail" that appears at the top of most course pages. It's called the breadcrumb trail because it can help you see how you arrived at your destination, and therefore can help you find your way back. Jump ahead to Figure 4.11 on page 29. Between the Tab area and the Announcement banner, you will see COURSES > APPLIED COMPUTER CONCEPTS–CISC 1301 > ANNOUNCE-MENTS. ANNOUNCEMENTS shows your current level in the system, and clicking the COURSES link will return you to the previous screen.

It's not a good idea to use the back and forward buttons located in the browser tool bar. In many instances, you will not reach your intended destination.

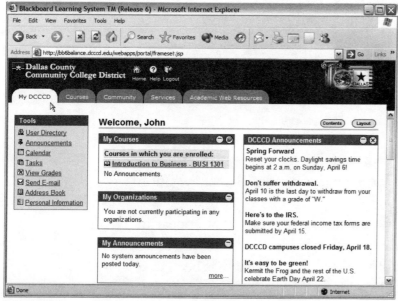

FIGURE 3.5

The My Institution tab has been customized by the systems administrator to say My DCCCD.

Customizing Blackboard

In some cases, you can customize the content boxes (also known as modules) that appear on your Blackboard tabs. If you look again at Figure 3.5, you will notice the My Courses, My Organizations, and My Announcements modules appear in the left panel under the Welcome John header, and DCCCD Announcements appear in the right panel. If you have a Contents button to the right of the header, you can add, move, and sometimes remove the modules that appear on this tab. You can also change the color of the title bars of the modules.

To Change the Modules

✔ Click the **Contents** button to the right of the header. (in Figure 3.5 this is located to the right of Welcome John).

✔ Click the check box to the left of each module that you would like to add to your page (see Figure 3.6).

✔ Scroll down to the bottom and click **Submit** for the changes to take effect.

✔ Click **OK** when "The page has successfully been customized" appears.

To Change the Arrangement of the Modules

✔ Click the **Layout** button (in Figure 3.5 this is located to the right of the Contents button).

✔ The **Customize Page Layout** option will appear (this is option number 1 in Figure 3.7).

✔ Click on the module you wish to rearrange.

✔ Click the up or down arrows at the right of the panels to move the option up or down within the panel.

✔ Modules can be removed from the left and right panels by clicking the red **X**.

✔ Modules with an asterisk (*) are permanent and cannot be removed.

✔ Scroll down and click **Submit** once you have completed your changes.

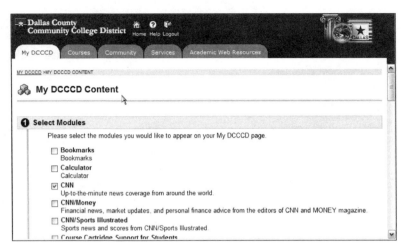

FIGURE 3.6
Click on the options you would like displayed in your left-hand frame.

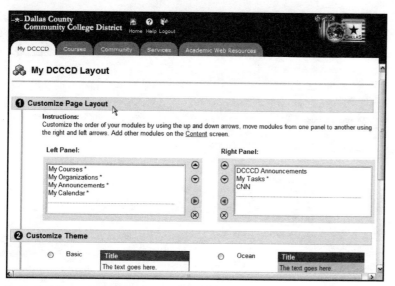

FIGURE 3.7 CUSTOMIZING BLACKBOARD.

TO CHANGE THE COLORS OF MODULES

Students may choose a theme from several different color options.

✔ Click the Layout button (in Figure 3.5 this is located to the right of the Contents button).

✔ The Customize Page Layout option will appear.

✔ Click the button to the left of the desired theme.

✔ In Figure 3.7, option number 2, Customize Theme, allows for eight different color variations. There may be a theme named for your college or university, or you can choose from combinations like ocean (shown), desert, fall, forest, spring, summer and winter.

✔ Scroll to the bottom and click the **Submit** button.

✔ Click **OK** when "The page has successfully been customized" appears.

Module 4 Navigating Blackboard

As you can see in Figure 4.1, Blackboard is divided into several areas. The top frame usually contains your college or university's logo, and Home, Help, and Login/Logout links. Below them is the tab region. Tabs may appear as My Institution, Courses, Community, Services, and Academic Web Resources, and the names may be customized to fit the needs of the institution. Each tab under this top frame leads to a different page, and most pages contain a navigation section (on the left side) and a main content area to the right.

My Institution

TOOLS

Depending on how your college or university has set up the system, you can use the Tools area to review announcements, calendar events, tasks, and grades for all courses. You will notice these links on the left-hand side of Figure 4.1 under Tools.

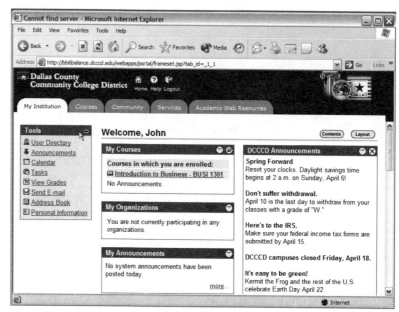

FIGURE 4.1
The Tools area, located on the left side of the window.

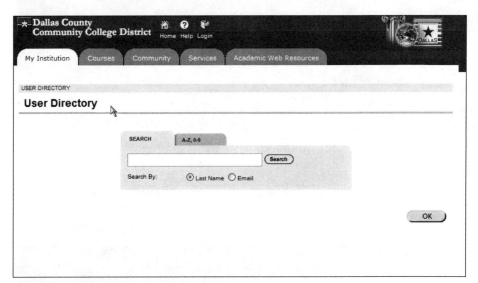

FIGURE 4.2 THE USER DIRECTORY.
By default, you will search the User Directory by Last Name.

USER DIRECTORY

If available, the user directory allows you to e-mail and view personal information about other users on Blackboard. Personal information can be viewed only if that person permits it. As a default setting, all user information is kept private. You must go into Personal Information (see Personal Information, p. 26) and set your information to Public for anyone to see that information. Only other people within the system—those people with a login—are allowed access to Personal Information.

Search. You can search for a person by Last Name or E-mail, or use the A-Z, 0-9 tab to retrieve an alphabetical list of all available users.

Tip. If you do not know the correct spelling, type in the first few letters that you do know, then click **Search**. You'll get a list of related spellings. In addition, if you want to view a list of all users, leave the text box blank and click the **Search** button. This step is not recommended due to the quantity of information that you will receive.

To return to the previous screen, click the **My Institution** tab, the **My Institution** link, or the **OK** button at the bottom of the page.

ANNOUNCEMENTS

By clicking **Announcements**, you can view all announcements in your current courses. For example, if you are taking biology, accounting, and history, this area would show all announcements for all three of these courses. You can modify how your announcements appear in two ways: the drop-down menu and the tab area.

Drop-Down Menu. You can choose an Announcements view from the drop-down menu on the right side of the page. The default is to Show All announcements from all your courses, but you can select a

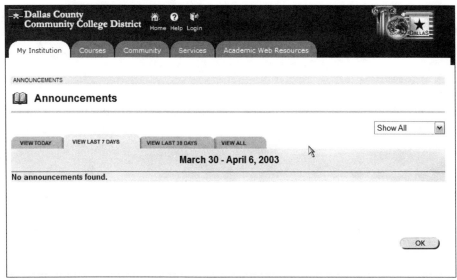

FIGURE 4.3 THE DROP-DOWN MENU.
Show All indicates that all announcements for all courses are given.

specific course with the drop-down menu to view the announcements from just that course.

Tab Area. This element enables you to select current or dated information. Tabs are arranged to View Today, View Last 7 Days, View Last 30 Days, and View All announcements. The default setting is View Last 7 Days.

To return to the previous screen, click the **My Institution tab**, the **My Institution link**, or the **OK** button at the bottom of the page.

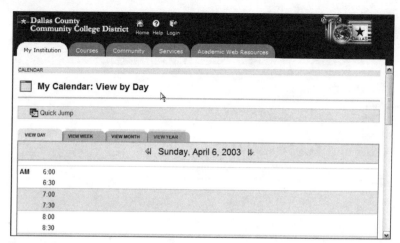

FIGURE 4.4
The View by Day tab is selected to show only one day's events.

CALENDAR

In Calendar you can view events for all classes on one calendar. Events may include the following:

✔ Course Events. For example, deadlines set by your instructor.

✔ Institutional Events. For example, information regarding drop dates or times when the system will be serviced.

Quick Jump. This button allows you to advance to a specific date in the past or future.

Tab Area. By clicking the calendar tabs, you can view items by day, week, month, or year. Clicking the dual arrows by the date allows the user to progress to the next or previous day.

To return to the previous screen, click the **My Institution** tab, the **My Institution** link, or the **OK** button at the bottom of the page.

TASKS

You could consider Tasks as a means to organize your work, much like an automated "To-Do" list. Instructors, system administrators, and you can add tasks throughout the term of the course. (See Figure 4.5.)

Add Task. To add a task, click the **Add Task** button. A screen will appear where you can add a Title and Description, set a Due Date, and note Priority and Status. Personal tasks you enter will fall under the My Tasks section of the drop-down menu.

Drop-Down Menu. This component allows you to view All Tasks, My Tasks, or tasks for a specific course.

View by Priority, Subject, Status, and Due Date. You can instantly arrange Tasks according to Priority, Subject, Status, and Due Date by clicking on the appropriate label.

To return to the previous screen, click the **My Institution** tab, the **My Institution** link, or the **OK** button at the bottom of the page.

VIEW GRADES

This area presents a grade for each of your Blackboard courses. Be aware, though, that not all schools/instructors will post grades to this area. Click on the listed course to view the grades related to that course. Obviously, this is a read-only area, and only the instructor or institution can add or modify content. (See Figure 4.6.)

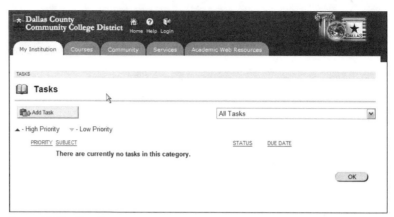

FIGURE 4.5 THE TASK SCREEN.

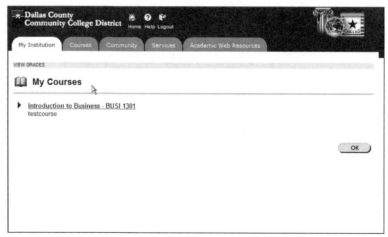

FIGURE 4.6 THE MY COURSES SCREEN.
To view your grades for a specific course, click on the appropriate course link.

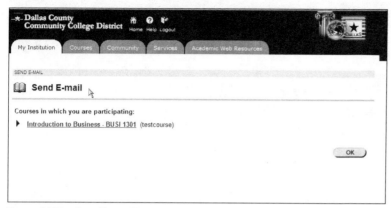

FIGURE 4.7 THE SEND E-MAIL SCREEN.
To send e-mail, you need to select a class link to retrieve an e-mail list for the people in that class.

To return to the previous screen, click the **My Institution tab**, the **My Institution link**, or the **OK** button at the bottom of the page.

SEND E-MAIL

This feature allows you to send e-mail within a specified course. *Note:* Some free e-mail systems have anti-spamming features that will inadvertently block e-mail sent from Blackboard to All Users or Groups of users because of the way Blackboard handles the addressing. E-mail sent to an individual is handled differently and would work appropriately. If you have questions concerning free e-mail accounts and Blackboard, contact your campus' technical support.

Course Links. By clicking the links for each of your courses you can jump directly to that course's Send E-mail page. E-mails can be sent to:

✔ **All Users.** Sends e-mail to all users in the course.

✔ **All Groups.** Sends e-mail to all of the instructor-created groups in a specified course.

✔ **All Teaching Assistants.** Sends e-mail to all of the teaching assistants in a specified course.

✔ **All Instructors.** Sends e-mail to all of the instructors for a specified course.

✔ **Select Users.** Sends e-mail to selected users in a specified course.

✔ **Select Groups.** Send e-mail to selected groups in a course.

By clicking the checkbox next to Send Copy of Message to self, you'll have a copy of any e-mail you send.

To return to the previous screen, click the **My Institution** tab, the **My Institution** link, or the **OK** button at the bottom of the page.

ADDRESS BOOK

Here you can add names and addresses to a personal list. Unlike Send E-mail and User Directory, only e-mail addresses that you personally add will appear in this section. No students or instructors are automatically added to this area.

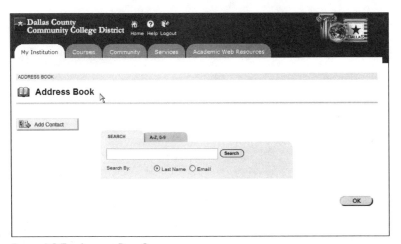

FIGURE 4.8 THE ADDRESS BOOK SCREEN.
To add a contact, click on the **Add Contact** button in the upper left corner of the window.

Add Contact. To add names and addresses, click the **Add Contact** button. Add the personal information of anyone you wish. This is your personal list and is not shared with anyone.

Search. You can search for a person by Last Name or E-mail, or use the A-Z, 0-9 tab to retrieve an alphabetical list of everyone you have added.

Tip. As with your User Directory, if you do not know the correct spelling, type in the first few letters that you know, then click **Search**. This will give you a list of related spellings. In addition, if you want to view a list of added users, leave the text box blank and click the **Search** button.

To return to the previous screen, click the **My Institution** tab, the **My Institution** link, or the **OK** button at the bottom of the page.

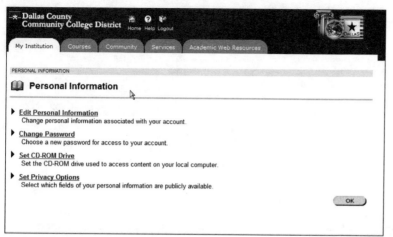

FIGURE 4.9 THE PERSONAL INFORMATION SCREEN.
Select **Edit Personal Information** to enter your e-mail address, and select **Set Privacy Options** to change your information from Private to Public.

PERSONAL INFORMATION

This should be the first area you visit after your first login. It is probably one of the most important areas within the system. Here you add or change personal information. You can make this information available or unavailable to other users.

Edit Personal Information. Add your e-mail address, home address, phone number, and other personal information to the system. It is very important to have your correct e-mail address. Your instructor will use this address to contact you. Free mail accounts may have trouble receiving some mails sent from Blackboard. Check with your technical support if you have any questions.

Change Password. Your Blackboard system may or may not allow you to change your password—in some cases, the password that Blackboard uses may be the password that your college or institution assigns for other campus systems. If you have the option to change your password, select a new password carefully and consider these points. First, it should be easy to remember. Second, do not write it down where anyone can find it. If you forget your password and your e-mail is in the system correctly, you can simply click the **Forgot Your Password?** link on the login screen, and an access URL will be immediately sent to your personal e-mail account. Third, choose a combination of numbers and letters for your password. A combination of numbers and letters is much more difficult to crack than only letters or only numbers if someone is trying to access your account.

Set CD-ROM Drive. This feature allows instructors to tie CD-ROM content to their course. This setting tells Blackboard which drive to look for once a CD is placed into your computer. Not all courses will use this function.

Set Privacy Options. When you register, your personal information is automatically considered private. **The system administrator and the instructor have access to your personal information whether or not you make it public.** You are able to select none, some, or all of your data to be open to the public. The options follow:

✔ E-mail address

✔ Address (street, city, state, zip, country)

✔ Work information (company, job title, work phone, work fax)

✔ Additional contact information (home phone, mobile phone, Web site) You may also choose to list your information in the user directory.

Courses Tab

The Courses tab lists the course you are taking, allows you access to the Blackboard catalog, lets you search for courses, and may offer a Web search tool.

Course List. This area displays all courses that you are registered in and that are in the Blackboard system. At the top you may notice it states: Courses you are teaching. If you were an instructor, your courses would be listed in this area, but since you are a student, your courses are listed under: Courses in which you are participating. You will also see the Course ID and name of the instructor for each of your courses. These items are important

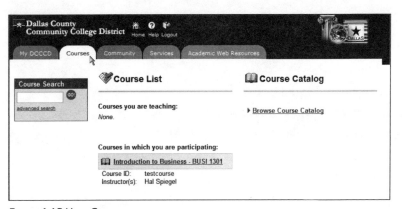

FIGURE 4.10 YOUR COURSE.
All your courses will be listed under the section Courses in which you are participating.

if you are reporting a problem about the course. To access your course, click the title of the course.

Course Catalog. Here you'll find the Blackboard catalog. Be aware that this catalog may not be identical to your college's catalog since some instructors may choose not to put their courses online. Some instructors allow parts of their course, like the syllabus, to be open so that students can sample course content and view the instructor's information.

Course Search. This allows students to directly search for courses that are in the catalog by title or course number.

ACCESSING A COURSE

To access your course, click on the course title link under: Course in which you are participating. The first page you'll see is usually the Announcements page. As the default, you can see announcements from the last 7 days, but you may choose other tab options as discussed in the Announcements section earlier in this chapter. The links or buttons to the left provide navigation to the course content. As in the rest of the system, the right panel displays the system content.

COLLAPSING THE COURSE'S NAVIGATION

In Figure 4.11, on the left side of the screen just above Announcements, you will see a small arrow. By clicking this arrow, the course navigation will collapse to allow for more screen space. See Figure 4.12 for an example.

COMMUNITY AND SERVICES TABS

Your system may have tabs for Community and Web Services (*Note*: these tabs may have different names). The Community area provides a place for on-campus and off-campus clubs and organizations to meet online.

The Services tab provides you with links to access student services online. Services might include online registration, parking information, important phone numbers, and so on.

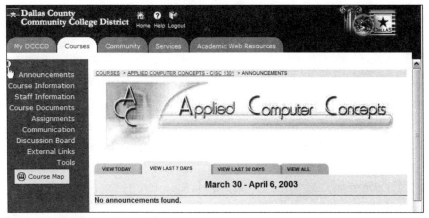

FIGURE 4.11 THE ANNOUNCEMENTS SCREEN.
The default view for announcements is: View Last 7 Days. You can change this by selecting one of the other views.

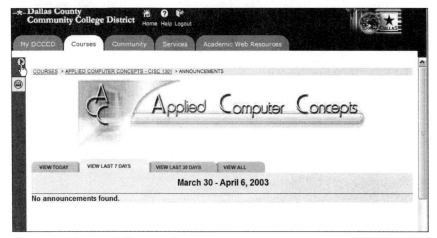

FIGURE 4.12 SCREEN WITH NAVIGATION COLLAPSED.
Click the arrow again and the screen will return to normal.

ACADEMIC WEB RESOURCES TAB

Some versions of Blackboard include an Academic Web Resources tab as shown in Figure 4.13.

If available, you can customize this feature to enhance your productivity. For example, if you are majoring in computer science, you can view resources on computer-related topics. For information on Academic Web Resources customization, click on **Help** located under Blackboard Resources (see Figure 4.14).

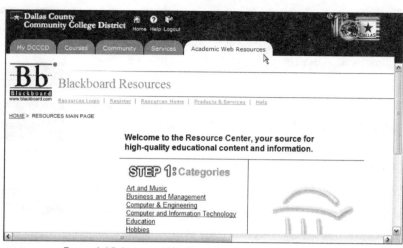

FIGURE 4.13 ACADEMIC WEB RESOURCES.
Connect here to a variety of resources related to your courses.

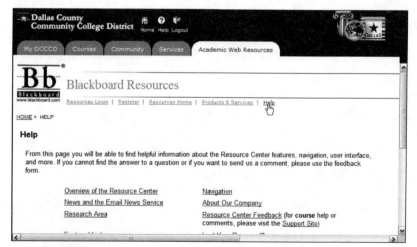

FIGURE 4.14
Click on **Help** for assistance with configuring Academic Web Resources.

Module 5 Course Content

Figure 5.1 shows the course level interface. As we stated earlier, navigation is listed vertically along the left-hand side while content appears in the right frame. The navigation links refer to parts of the course. Courses vary: Navigation links may be worded differently, they may appear in different colors, they may not appear at all, or may be graphically represented as buttons. It's up to the individual instructor.

Links that you may see are

✔ Announcements
✔ Course Information
✔ Staff Information
✔ Course Documents
✔ Assignments
✔ Communication
✔ Discussion Board
✔ External Links
✔ Tools

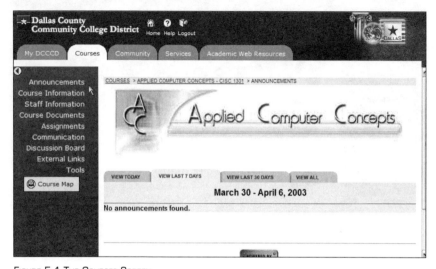

FIGURE 5.1 THE COURSES SCREEN.
By default, Announcements will appear when you enter your course.

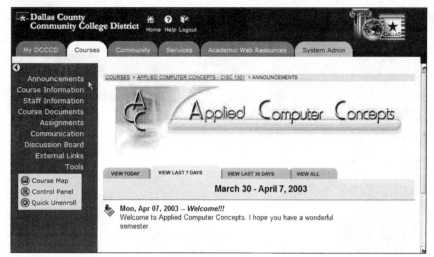

FIGURE 5.2 THE ANNOUNCEMENTS SCREEN.
You can return to the Announcements page at any time by clicking the **Announcements** button on the left side of the window.

Announcements

Announcements are usually the top link, and the Announcements page is often the course main page. From this page you have access to all current course and system news. Many institutions use this feature to inform students of campus closings for inclement weather, information on upcoming events, and the like.

The default view is to show announcements that have occurred in the last 7 days. The user can choose to view information that was entered today only, within the last 7 days, within the last 30 days, or all announcements. Announcements that the institution or administrator set as permanent will always show and will be listed first.

You may be wondering, what is the difference between this announcements area and the one discussed in the Tools section? This Announcement area—the area under the Courses tab—shows only system announcements and announcement that pertain to the particular course, while the other Announcement area combines all announcements, including announcements from other courses.

Course Information

The instructor may put any electronic information in the Course Information area. You may find course orientation material, a syllabus, content specifics about the course, and possibly computer setup requirements.

Staff Information

This area gives you information on the course instructor. Professors can choose to have their name, phone number, office location, and office hours displayed here. They may even have a picture of themselves.

Course Documents

This is another course content area, and the instructor may display any electronically formatted information here. You may find chapter information, electronic books, multimedia demonstrations, video, and audio. (See Figure 5.5.)

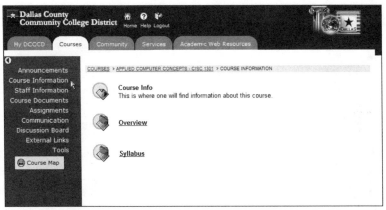

FIGURE 5.3 COURSE INFORMATION.
Clicking on the **Course Information** button usually provides information such as the course syllabus and orientation.

FIGURE 5.4 STAFF INFORMATION.
Here you'll find valuable contact information about your instructor.

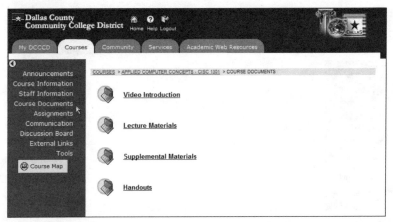

FIGURE 5.5 COURSE DOCUMENTS.
Click the **Course Documents** button to view content your instructor has uploaded. Your button styles and names may appear different from what is shown here because the instructor can customize the buttons.

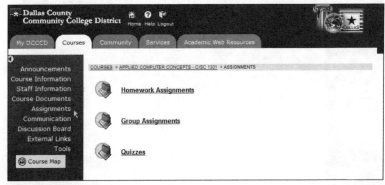

FIGURE 5.6 ASSIGNMENTS.
You may find labs, assignments, and tests here.

Some documents may not display initially on your computer. For example, an instructor may have a PowerPoint presentation uploaded for you to view. If you do not have PowerPoint installed on your computer, the file will not play. In this case you will need to go to http://www.microsoft.com and download the free PowerPoint viewer. If you have any questions concerning software required for your course, contact your instructor.

Assignments

Assignments is yet another content area. (See Figure 5.6.) Electronic content is displayed in this locale. You may find labs, assignments, and tests here, although tests may appear in any of the content areas.

In the Assignments area, you are likely to find an automated assessment, such as a quiz. In Blackboard, some quizzes can be graded instantly to provide you with feedback. This feature may also offer practice quizzes, which have no point value. Quizzes may be listed individually, as in Figure 5.7, or in a folder.

TO TAKE A QUIZ

✔ First, Click the **Quizzes** link or button.

You will be prompted with: Are you sure you want to take this assessment now? (Figure 5.8.) Be careful. Some tests are set so that you can take them only once. If you click OK, that means you are ready to take the test. If you are not ready and you click OK, you will have to contact your instructor and have that person reset your test. If you are not ready to take the test, click Cancel, and you can come back to it when you are ready.

✔ Click **OK** if you are ready.

✔ Next, your quiz will be displayed. Look in the status bar, and a counter will display if the quiz is timed. Do not surf the Internet in the same browser you are using to take the test. This may break the connection with the server, and you may not be able to submit the test. If you need to look up information while taking a test, open another browser. (To open a new browser in Internet Explorer, go to the browser's file menu and select **New Window**. In Netscape, hold down the Control key (**Ctrl**) and press the **N** key.)

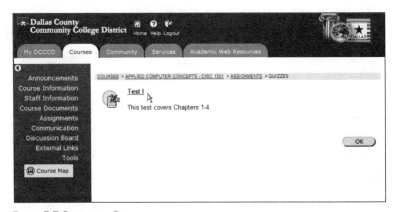

FIGURE 5.7 CHOOSING A QUIZ.
Quizzes may appear under a button like Assignments, or you may see a link to a quiz in the Announcements area.

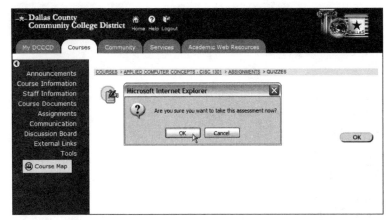

FIGURE 5.8 TAKING A QUIZ.
Click OK only if you are ready to take the test. Clicking OK prematurely may block you from taking the quiz.

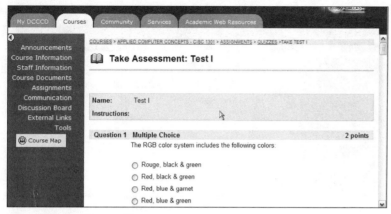

FIGURE 5.9 SUBMITTING THE QUIZ.
When taking a quiz be sure to scroll down to see all the questions. Your quiz will not be graded unless you scroll to the bottom and click the **Submit** button.

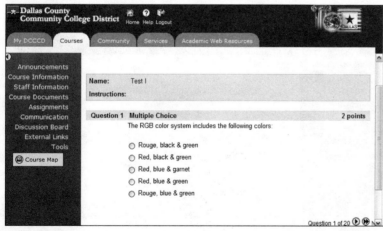

FIGURE 5.10
The single arrow moves you to the next question and the double arrow moves you to the end of the test. Scroll down and click **Submit** when you are finished taking your test.

✔ Once you have completed the test, scroll to the bottom and click the **Submit** button. If you do not click Submit, your results will not be sent to the server and there will be no grade. If you lose your Internet connection while taking a test, your test may not be submitted and you may need to contact your instructor to reset the test. If you have problems, try taking the test again before contacting your instructor.

Instructors may choose to have the questions displayed all at once or one at a time. Figure 5.9 displays questions presented all at once and Figure 5.10 shows questions displayed one at a time. Both pictures look similar but their functionality is different. When questions are displayed one at a time, you must navigate through the questions one at a time using the arrows at the bottom right-hand side of the screen. You may need to scroll down to see the arrows. The single arrow moves you to the next question and the double arrow moves you to the end of the test.

Communication and Discussion Board

Communication will be discussed in Module 6. Discussion Board allows you a means to access discussion questions from a button link instead of clicking on the Communications button and locating the Discussion Board in that area.

As always, these links can be customized and may not be available.

External links

External links (Figure 5.11) can take you to related Internet links. Along with the link to the site, you'll see the URL and a short description of the site. External links can also appear in other content areas.

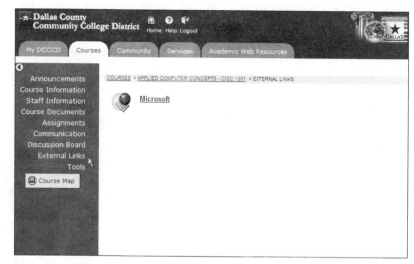

FIGURE 5.11 EXTERNAL LINKS.
When the link is clicked, the site may appear within the Blackboard frame or may open a new browser window.

Blackboard provides you with three different tools to communicate with faculty and other students. They are

✔ Send E-mail
✔ Collaboration
✔ Discussion Board

There may be other student tools available under a link to Communication; your instructor can decide which tools you have access to. Announcements are the

FIGURE 6.1 COMMUNICATION.
Click the **Communication** link to access Blackboard's communication tools.

same as discussed earlier in this text. If you click the Announcements, it brings you to the Announcements section (see Figure 5.2 on page 32 for an example). Roster displays a list of all the other students in your course, and Group Pages displays group information. Groups must be set up by the instructor for this information to be displayed.

E-mail

This e-mail is the same e-mail component discussed under Tools on Module 4 on page 24. You can send e-mail in the follow ways:

✔ **All Users.** Sends e-mail to all students, and instructors in the course.

✔ **All Groups.** Sends e-mail to all of the groups in a specified course.

✔ **All Teaching Assistants.** Sends e-mail to all of the teaching assistants in a specified course.

✔ **All Instructors.** Sends e-mail to all of the instructors for a specified course.

✔ **All Observers.** Sends e-mail to all persons set with observer status in this course. Not active in Figure 6.2.

✔ **Select Users.** Sends e-mail to selected users in a specified course.

✔ **Select Groups.** Send e-mail to selected groups in a course.

✔ **Selected Observers.** Sends e-mail to selected observers in a specified course. Not active in Figure 6.2.

By clicking the checkbox next to Send Copy of Message to self, you have the ability to copy yourself on any e-mail you send. Click **Add** to attach a document to your e-mail. Click **Submit** to send your e-mail. (See Figure 6.3.)

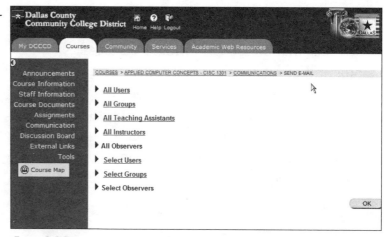

FIGURE 6.2 E-MAIL.
You can send E-mail to others in your course.

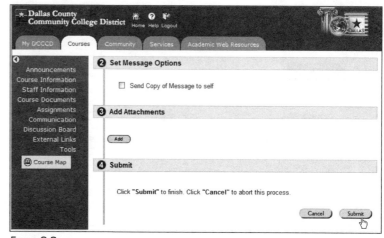

FIGURE 6.3
Scroll down to the bottom and click **Submit** to send your e-mail.

Collaboration

The Collaboration tool can contain Virtual Classrooms and/or Lightweight Chat sessions. Collaboration is a synchronous discussion tool. This means that all participants are logged on the system simultaneously. Communication is happening live and users are able to see responses as they are sent. (See Figure 6.4.)

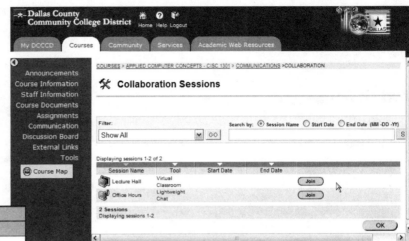

FIGURE 6.4

Click **Join** to enter the Virtual Classroom or Lightweight Chat. The Virtual Classroom contains all the functionality of Lightweight Chat, plus some additional tools like a Course Map, Whiteboard, and Group Browser.

VIEW, CLEAR, AND BREAKOUT TOOL BAR

Located at the top of the screen (see Figure 6.5), View allows you to specify how private messages are displayed. Clear allows you to clear the screen, and Breakout enables students to go to sub chat sessions.

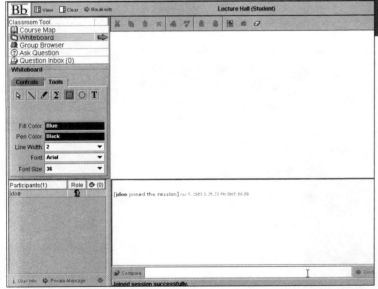

FIGURE 6.5 THE BLACKBOARD VIRTUAL CLASSROOM.

Virtual Classroom Tools

Course Map. Displays a map of the content of the Blackboard course and allows you to access content while in a chat session.

Whiteboard. Allows students and instructors to draw, type, or add graphics into the main screen.

Group Browser. Enables students and instructors to navigate the Web while in chat session.

Ask Questions. Private questions can be sent to other students or the instructor.

Question Inbox. Displays questions sent to students or instructors.

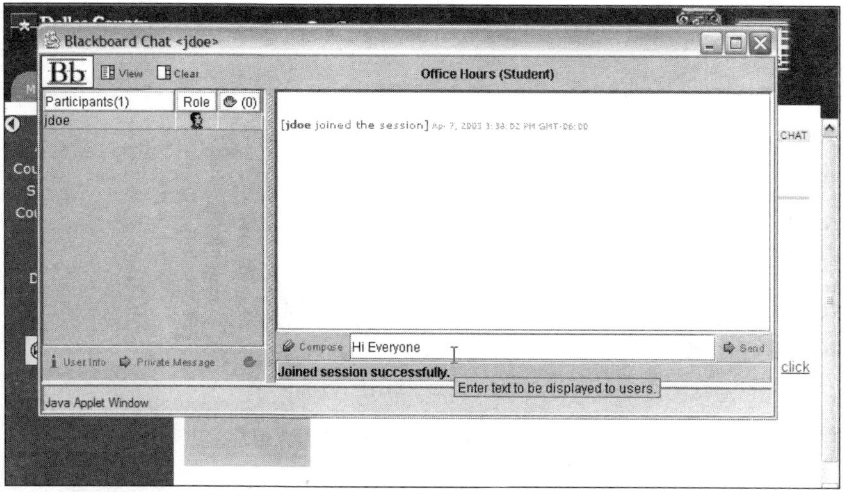

FIGURE 6.6 LIGHTWEIGHT CHAT.
"Hi Everyone" is entered in the Compose area. When Enter is pressed on your keyboard, the message is displayed to everyone.

Chat Area. Near the bottom of Figure 6.5, you will see an area labeled Compose. This area is the text-based chat component. Next to this you will see a one-line text box. This text area is where you can write your questions and comments. To submit your questions and comments, click **Send** (or press **Enter** on keyboard). Within seconds, you will see what you wrote in the above text area. This message will appear on the screens of all users logged into the virtual chat. This works the same for Lightweight Chat. In Figure 6.6, "Hi Everyone" is displayed in the Compose text area. When Enter is pressed on the keyboard, you will see "jdoe said 'Hi Everyone.'" The Participants box on the left side on the screen (the lower left in Figure 6.5) shows all users logged on to the chat session.

Discussion Boards

Discussion boards offer asynchronous communication. This means that an instructor or student can post a topic and you can respond in a few minutes, several hours, or a month from now (but before the due date!). All users do not need to be simultaneously logged in to participate.

Discussion Boards is a threaded discussion forum. This means that a person can create a new question (sometimes called a thread) if

FIGURE 6.7 MORE COMMUNICATION.
Click the **Discussion Boards** link to access the Discussion area. This link and the Discussion Board link in the left-hand panel are the same.

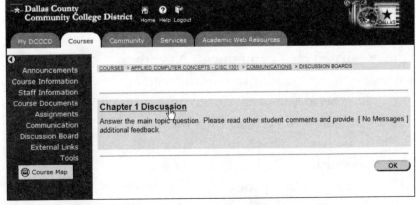

FIGURE 6.8 THE DISCUSSION BOARD.
Click the underlined text or the link (in this example, Chapter 1 Discussion) to view the discussion area for the forum.

permitted by the instructor or respond to an existing question.

First, click on the **Discussion Boards** link. This will display the discussion topics. Next, click on the topic of your choice. For example, in Figure 6.8 you see that "Chapter 1" is the topic. This link, not the OK button, must be clicked to access this discussion area. The OK button will bring you back to the previous page.

This will bring you to the Threaded Discussion area where you will find the following:

✔ **Add New Thread**. By clicking this button you can add new threads. *Note*: The instructor may choose to turn off this feature.

✔ **Discussion Topic**. Clicking this link gives you the chance to display the threads and respond to them. In Figure 6.9 the topic is "Topic 1."

✔ **Question or Response Originator**. By clicking this link you can e-mail the author directly.

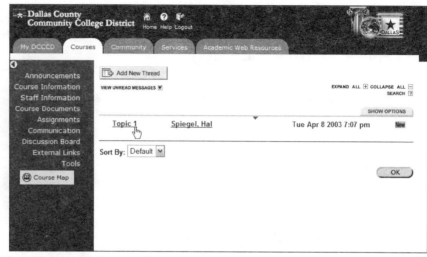

FIGURE 6.9 ANOTHER DISCUSSION BOARD.
Click the underlined text or link (in this example, "Topic 1") to view the question or comment.

✔ **Show Options**. Here you can select or deselect threads, mark them as read or unread, or collect them to display on a single page. You must select the messages by placing a check in the check box to the left before you can mark them as read or collect them to display on a single page.

✔ **Expand All, Collapse All, and Search**. You can expand the list and collapse the area for easier navigation. Search allows you to explore the area for key words.

✔ **Sort**. You can sort by Author, Date, or Subject.

Once you click the **Topic** link, the question will appear. To reply to the question or statement, click the **Reply** button. (See Figure 6.10.)

After you click **Reply**, respond to the question and click **Submit**. Your response will appear as a subset to the original thread. (See Figure 6.11.)

When you send a response, the Subject automatically appears. Next, you can type a message, in plain text or HTML. Smart Text means that you will add a few basic HTML tags, like <B> </B> for

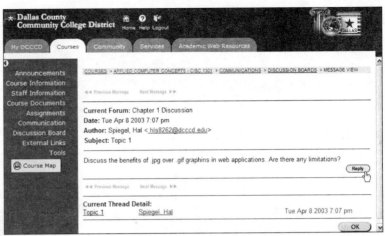

FIGURE 6.10 PARTICIPATING IN THE DISCUSSION.
Click the **Reply** button to respond to the question.

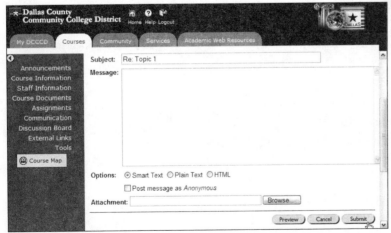

FIGURE 6.11 THE MESSAGE BOX.
Prepare you response in the message box and click **Submit** to respond to the question or comment.

bold, <I> </I> for italics, <BR> for a line break and so on, for formatting purposes.

You may choose to post an Anonymous response, which means your name will not appear next to your comments. Your instructor may disable this feature.

If you have electronic material like a PowerPoint presentation or PDF file that can support your statements, you may attach it to your statement.

After you have completed your response, you may click Preview to double-check your work or click Submit to send the information to the server.

Blackboard has other tools, and the instructor will decide which tools you can use. Click on the **Tools** button and you may see:

✔ Digital Drop Box
✔ Edit Your Homepage
✔ Personal Information
✔ Calendar
✔ View Grades
✔ Student Manual (not shown)
✔ Tasks (not shown)
✔ Electronic Blackboard (not shown)
✔ Address Book (not shown)

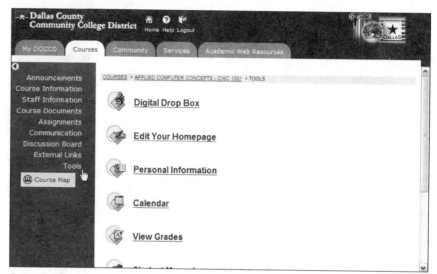

FIGURE 7.1 TOOLS.
Click the **Tools** button to access Blackboard's student tools.

   In the upcoming section, we will discuss Digital Drop Box, Edit Your Homepage, and Electronic Blackboard. Personal Information, Calendar, Check Grade, Tasks, and Address Book have been discussed previously.

Digital Drop Box

This tool lets you save documents to the server and to submit electronic homework files to your professor. You may be asked to use this function as your personal storage space on the server for your homework and other documents.

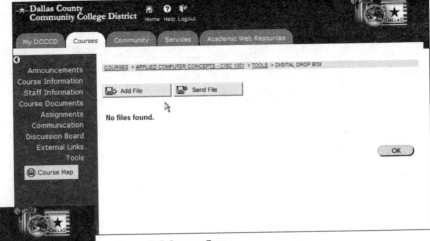

FIGURE 7.2 SENDING FILES
Click the **Add File** button to upload the file to the server. Click the **Send File** button to send the file to the instructor.

First, upload a document to the server. Click the **Add File** button (see Figure 7.2).

Next, you will be prompted with several text-entry boxes (see Figure 7.3).

✔ Title:

✔ File:

✔ Comments:

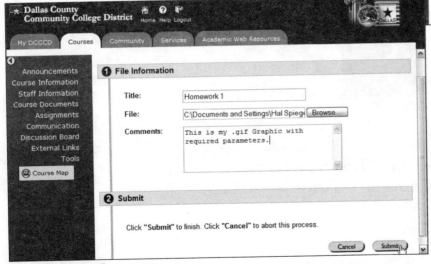

FIGURE 7.3 ADDING A FILE.
Click the **Browse** button to search your hard drive or floppy to find the file you want to add.

It is a good practice to include a file title that describes the submitted document well. It will make future reference to the document easier for your instructor and you.

To add a file, click the **Browse** button. This allows you to search your hard drive and select the appropriate document.

The comments section gives you the chance to send additional information to the instructor along with the document.

To upload to the server, scroll to the bottom and click **Submit**.

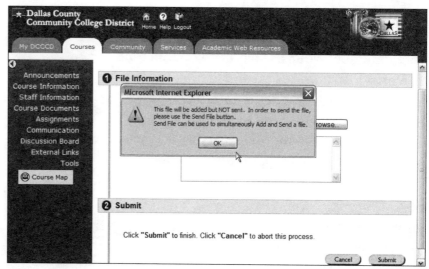

FIGURE 7.4
Click **OK** and the document will be uploaded to the server.

Next, you will be prompted with an alert box to warn you that the document resides only on the server at this time and has not been sent to your instructor (Figure 7.4).

Next you will receive a "Receipt: Success" to inform you the your document was successfully sent to the server (Figure 7.5). Click **OK** to continue. If this receipt is not received, a

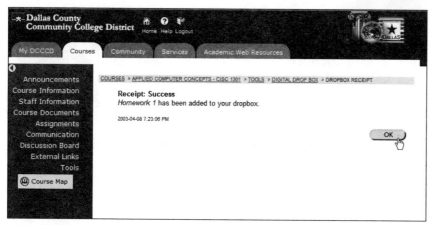

FIGURE 7.5 RECEIPT SUCCESS.
The document was uploaded to the server. Click **OK** to continue.

problem probably occurred in the process and your document did not upload.

Remember, your file has not yet been sent to your instructor. To send a file to your instructor, click the **Send File** button. (See Figure 7.6.) Documents can be sent only to your instructor's digital drop box. Documents can be sent that have already been

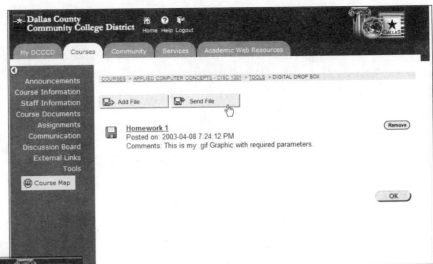

FIGURE 7.6
Click **Send File** to send Homework 1 or another file to your instructor.

uploaded to the server or sent directly from your own computer.

To send a file that was previously uploaded, click the down arrow in the Select file text box and choose the file you wish to submit (Figure7.7). Click **Submit** to send the file (Figure 7.8).

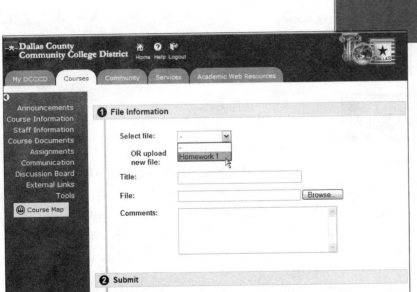

FIGURE 7.7 SELECT FILE.
Homework 1 is available to be sent to your instructor.

If you want to send a file directly to your instructor without adding it first, click the **Browse** button and select the file from your hard drive that you wish to send.

Look at the difference between Homework 2 and Homework 1 (Figure 7.9). Homework 1 has a Remove button to the right and Homework 2 does not. This means that Homework 2 has been sent to your instructor and Homework 1 has not been sent.

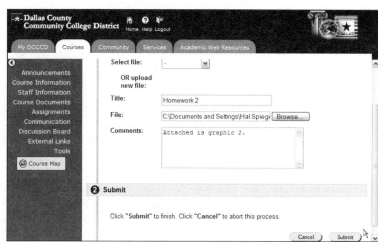

FIGURE 7.8
Click **Submit** to send the file.

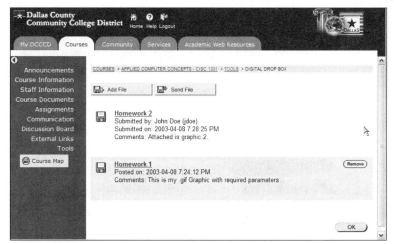

FIGURE 7.9
Added documents can be removed and sent documents cannot.

When documents are sent, only your instructor can remove them from the server. If you add a document to the server, you can use the Digital Drop Box as your own storage space. You can remove the document or send it to your instructor at a later date.

Edit Your Homepage

The Edit Your Homepage link allows students to add a personalized Web page to the system. Even without knowing any HTML, you can create a personal Web page with text, graphics, and links. This page becomes part of the entire the system, so when you create it for one course, it will appear in all courses.

First, click on the **Edit Your Homepage** link. (See Figure 7.10.)

Next, text entry boxes will appear (Figure 7.11). These areas are

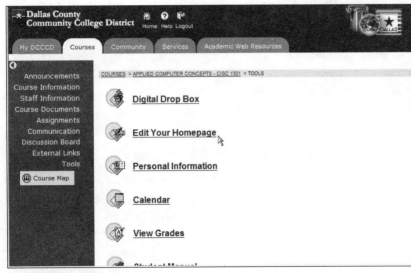

✔Intro Message
✔Personal Information
✔New Image
✔Site 1 Title
✔Site 1 URL
✔Description
✔Site 2 Title
✔Site 2 URL
✔Description
✔Site 3 Title
✔Site 3 URL
✔Description

FIGURE 7.10 EDITING YOUR HOMEPAGE.
Click **Edit Your Homepage** to add and modify your personal homepage.

The Intro Message and Personal Information are plain-text fields. This means that anything you type will appear in that area. Because it is plain text, advanced formatting will not appear (for example, different fonts, bold text, and so on are not available).

In the area on the window labeled "2 Upload a Picture," you may upload a single graphic. Click the **Browse** button to search your personal hard drive. (*Note*: Graphics need to be in JPEG or GIF format to be viewed over the Internet.)

Favorite Web Sites (not shown in Figure 7.11), allows you to add Web links to your homepage. You must add the full http://

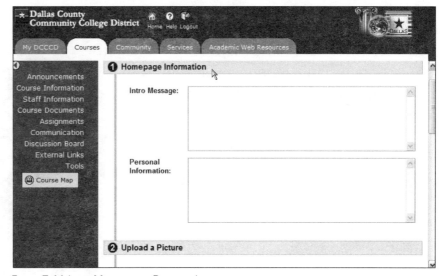

FIGURE 7.11 INTRO MESSAGE AND PERSONAL INFORMATION.
These are only a few options that you can enter in your personal homepage.

protocol for the link to function. For example, if you wanted to create a link to Microsoft's Web site, you would need to write **http://www.microsoft.com**.

As always, click the **Submit** button to upload your work.

Electronic Blackboard

The Electronic Blackboard is an electronic note-taking system. This component allows you to take notes and access them from anywhere you can access the Blackboard system.

First, click on the **Electronic Blackboard** link.

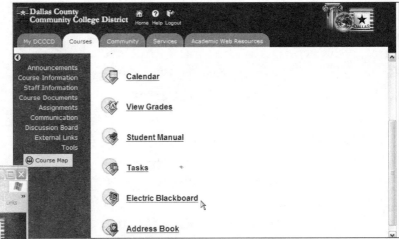

FIGURE 7.12 ELECTRONIC BLACKBOARD.
Click **Electronic Blackboard** for the electronic notes area to appear.

Next, the Electric Blackboard text box will appear. After you type your notes, click **Submit**, and your notes are saved to the system (Figure 7.13). This is a text-only area, so graphics and text formatting are not available. You must type all your notes into one document. They cannot be split into separate files, so you cannot have a file for Chapter 1 notes and another for Chapter 2 notes.

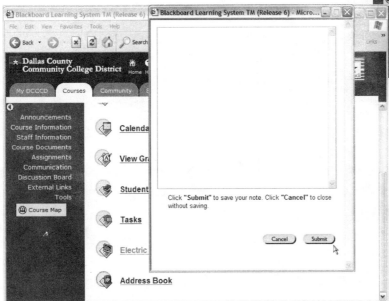

FIGURE 7.13 SAVING NOTES.
Adding text to the Electronic Blackboard text area allows you to save notes within a course.

The Blackboard Manual

Blackboard provides a Blackboard Student Manual through the Tools button. Note that your instructor or systems administrator can disable this feature. If you do not see this feature, contact your instructor.

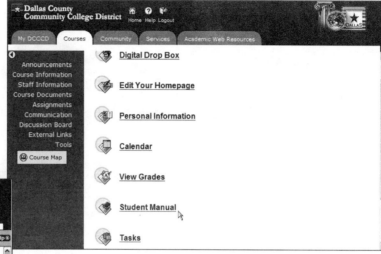

To access the Manual, click the **Student Manual link.**

Next, the online manual will appear. You can review the Contents or use the Search feature. When searching by content, click the **Contents** tab.

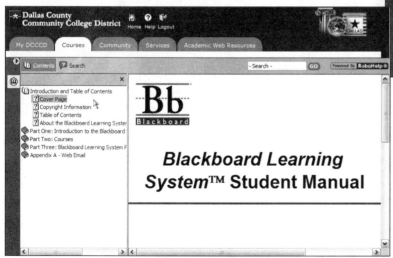

FIGURE 8.2 BLACKBOARD'S INTERNAL STUDENT MANUAL.
Collapse the left-hand frame to view more of the screen.

Next, click the closed book icon to expand the subject areas. Click the titles to display each section in the right-hand frame.

To use the Search feature, click the **Search** tab. Type in the key words to search for. Press **Enter**, and matched results will appear in the text area.

Blackboard Homepage

Blackboard's main Web site is located at: **http://www.blackboard.com.** This site offers general information about the system and links to support

Additional Internet Help Sites

✔ Internet Search Engines
- **http://www.google.com**
- **http://www.altavista.com**
- **http://www.lycos.com**
- **http://www.msn.com**

✔ Free E-mail Accounts
- **http://www.hotmail.com**
- **http://www.juno.com**

FIGURE 8.3 BLACKBOARD'S HOMEPAGE SHOWING SUPPORT TAB.

✔ Free Software
- http://www.download.com
- http://www.shareware.com

✔ Plugins
- http://www.real.com (Real Media)
- http://www.macromedia.com (Flash, Shockwave)
- http://www.microsoft.com (PowerPoint Viewer)

✔ Support
- http://support.blackboard.com

✔ Blackboard's ADA Information
- http://www.blackboard.com/products/access/index.htm

Frequently Asked Questions about Blackboard

Q. How do I access my Blackboard?

A. Contact your instructor or registrar to get the URL for your campus's Blackboard system. Many institutions have Web sites that list their Blackboard's site and provide login and orientation information.

Q. What are the minimum system requirements?

A. The basic rule of thumb: If your computer can run Internet Explorer 4 or higher, or Netscape 4 or higher, then you can use Blackboard. Obviously, the faster your system, the better your system will perform. We highly recommend that you use a multimedia computer system to receive the most from your courseware.

Q. Will Blackboard work on both Mac and PC operating systems?

A. Yes, Blackboard is designed to work cross-platform.

Q. Can my username and password be changed?

A. Your username cannot be changed, but your password usually can. See Module 4 under Personal Information for instructions on how to perform this task.

			Microsoft® Internet Explorer						Netscape® Navigator®					
			4.5	5.0	5.1	5.2	5.5	6.0	4.8	4.8	6.0	6.1	6.2	7.0
Blackboard Learning and Community Portal Systems™ (Release 6.0)	Microsoft Windows®	Windows 2000	X				X	X	X					
		Windows XP						X					X	X
	Apple® Macintosh®	Mac® OS 9.2	X	X						X				X
		Mac OS X.1			X	X						X	X	
		Mac OS X.2						X						X
Blackboard Learning System ML™	Microsoft Windows	Windows 2000					X		X					
	Apple Macintosh	Mac OS X.1				X							X	
Blackboard Learning System™ (Release 5.6)	Microsoft Windows	Windows 2000	X				X	X	X	X		X		
	Apple Macintosh	Mac OS 9.2			X	X				X	X	X		
		Mac OS X.1			X	X					X	X		
Blackboard 5™ (Release 5.5.1)	Microsoft Windows	Windows NT	X							X				
		Windows 2000	X	X		X			X		X			
	Apple Macintosh	Mac OS 9.1	X	X					X	X	X			

FIGURE 8.4

Above is a list of recommended/tested browser versions. Graphic courtesy of http://www.blackboard.com.

Q. What is the optimum screen resolution for viewing Blackboard?

A. Blackboard is best viewed at a screen resolution of 800 x 600 or greater.

Q. Is one browser better to use than another?

A. Blackboard works with both Netscape and Internet Explorer.

Q. Will Blackboard work without a connection to the Internet?

A. This system is Web-based and requires an Internet connection.

Q. How do I get technical help?

A. Institutions usually provide technical support. Check your campus' Web site. If you cannot get the help you need, your instructor should be able provide you with the e-mail address or phone number of someone who can help you.

Q. Is Blackboard ADA and section 508 compliant?

A. Basically yes, but go to **http://www.blackboard.com/products/access/index.htm** for additional information.

Q. How do I find an Internet Service Provider?

A. Start by contacting your college's technical support, which can provide you with a list of local providers that meet your needs.

Blackboard 5 is a previous release to the Blackboard 6 E-Learning system. It was the original release of the enterprise level software. Blackboard 5's look and feel is somewhat different but its functionality is similar.

This appendix is designed to demonstrate the differences in the two versions of the software. The first question that you are probably asking is which version of the software is my campus using? There is one easy way to tell. Go back and look at Figures 4.11 and 4.12 on page 29. Remember the button on the left side of the screen that you use to expand and contract the screen width? This feature is available only in Blackboard 6. The arrows are permanent and are not removable. Blackboard 5 does not have this feature. To check your campus version, log in, click on the **Courses** tab, and go into any of your courses. If you see the arrow (as in Figures 4.11 and 4.12), the version you are using is Blackboard 6 and you will not need to refer to this appendix. If the arrows are not available to you, the version you are using is Blackboard 5, and this section will be very important.

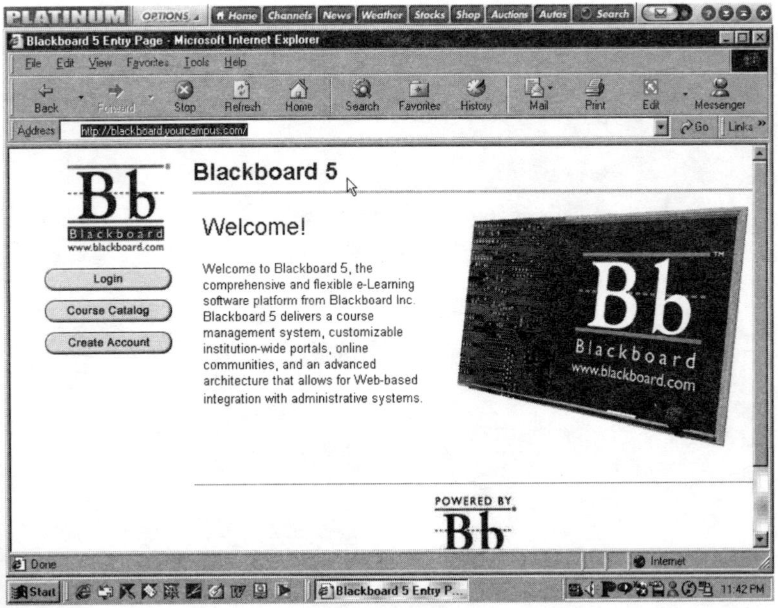

Figure A.1 is Blackboard 5's default login page. This page is highly customizable and is usually set

FIGURE A.1
Blackboard Login Screen. Your login screen may look different.

up with your school's logo and has information specific to its installation. As a general rule, you will always see a **Login** button.

After you click the **Login** button, you will be prompted for your username and password. (See Figure A.2.)

As in Blackboard 6, the login and password that you use allows Blackboard to recognize you as a unique person within the system. When you take a test, submit a document, or answer a discussion question, Blackboard attaches your identification to the transaction. Anytime you do anything on the system, your actions are tracked. Keep your username and password secure; do not give them to anyone.

The **Forgot your password?** option is also available. An e-mail will be sent to you with a URL that will grant you temporary access and allow you to reset your password under the Personal Information option.

Enter your username and password, then click **Login**. If you do not know your username and password, contact the instructor or the registrar's office.

Blackboard Gateway

Once you have clicked **Login**, the Blackboard Gateway appears. In Blackboard 5, there are two

FIGURE A.2 THE BLACKBOARD 5 DEFAULT WELCOME SCREEN.
After you enter your username and password, click the **Login** button.

Blackboard 5.0

interface options that institutions can display. Either they can have only a course management system (Figure A.3), or they can have a course management system and an educational portal (Figure A.4).

Blackboard refers to the course management system as the *Basic Learning System* and to the course management system and education portal as

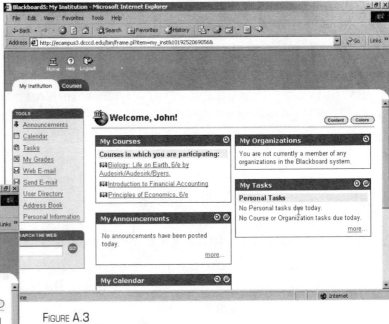

FIGURE A.3
Blackboard with only the course management system.

the *Learning System and Portal*. The Basic Learning System delivers a specific course's content to you, while the Learning System and Portal offers an educational entryway to a multitude of educational content and materials. The Learning System and Portal setup allows you to research questions and ideas beyond the scope of the normal course.

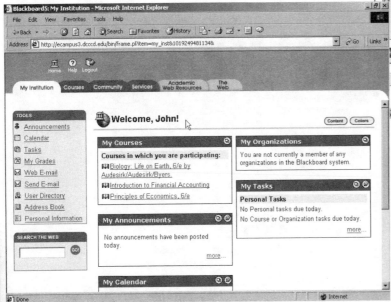

FIGURE A.4
Blackboard with the course management system and an educational portal.

Navigating Blackboard

After you log in, navigating the system is the same for both version 5 and 6. Tabs are located across the top; the left side of the screen provides navigation; and the right-hand frame is where the content appears.

Navigation is less customizable by the instructor in Blackboard 5, so the system may feel a little more uniform to you than Blackboard 6.

Customizing Blackboard

Customizing Blackboard 5 is a little different than in Blackboard 6. You may customize modules under the My Institution tab. Look again at Figure A.4. The modules show up under "Welcome, John!" My Courses, My Announcements, My

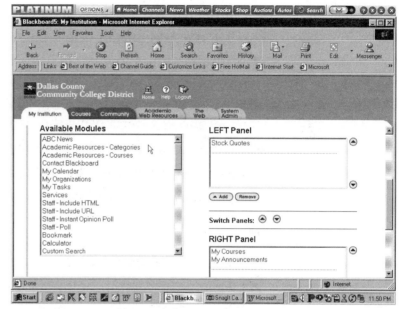

FIGURE A.5 CUSTOMIZING BLACKBOARD.
Highlight the desired module, and click the **Add** button to add it to the left or right panel.

Calendar appear in the left panel, and My Organizations and My Tasks appear in the right panel. You may add, move, and sometimes remove these modules. You can also change the color of the title bars of the modules.

To customize this area

✔ Click the **Contents** button to the right of your name (in Figure A.4 this button is located to the right of "Welcome, John!").

✔ The personalizing page layout screen will appear as in Figure A.5.

✔ On the left side, click on the item you wish to add. This will highlight the option.

✔ Click the **Add** button below the right or left panel to move the module to that area.

✔ With the option highlighted, click the up or down arrows at the right of the panels to move the option up or down within the panel.

✔ With the option highlighted, you can move the module from the right panel to the left panel and vice-versa using the arrows located between the two panels.

✔ Modules can be removed from the panels by clicking the **Remove** button.

✔ Modules with an asterisk (*) are permanent and cannot be removed.

✔ Scroll down and click **Submit** once you have completed your changes.

To change the color

✔ Click the **Colors** button to the right on the Contents button (SeeFigure A.4.)

✔ Click on the color from the color pallete.

✔ Click **Submit**, and the color in the title bars of each module is changed.

My Institution

Tools

Tools are identical in Blackboard 5 and 6. As you may recall, depending on how your college or university has set up the system, you can use the Tools area to review Announcements, Calendar Events, Tasks, and Grades for all courses. You will notice these links on the left-hand side of Figure A.6. If you have any questions about the tools area, refer to Module 4.

Courses Tab

One additional feature that Blackboard 5 has is a "Search the Web" feature. Look on the left-hand

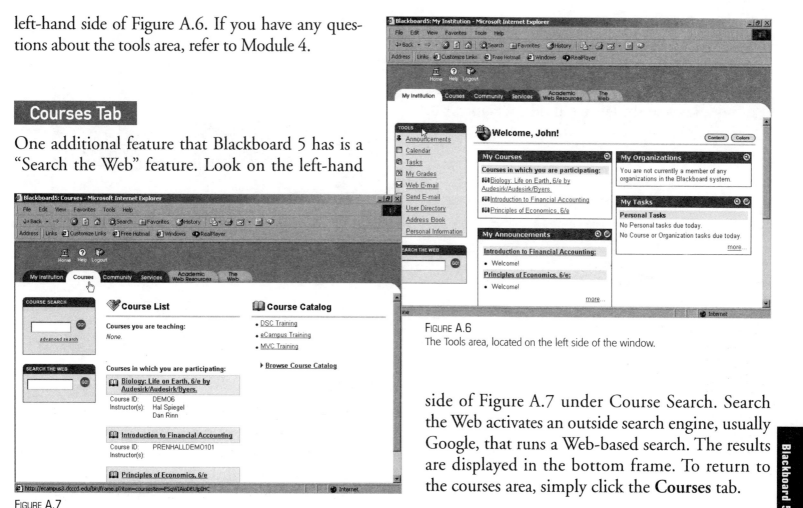

FIGURE A.6
The Tools area, located on the left side of the window.

FIGURE A.7
Search the Web, unique to Blackboard 5.

side of Figure A.7 under Course Search. Search the Web activates an outside search engine, usually Google, that runs a Web-based search. The results are displayed in the bottom frame. To return to the courses area, simply click the **Courses** tab.

ACCESSING A COURSE

Course navigation is similar in both Blackboard 5 and 6. Blackboard 5 offers only navigation buttons, and Blackboard 6 will either have buttons or text links. Look at the left-hand side of Figure A.8. There is no arrow for expanding and contracting the screen.

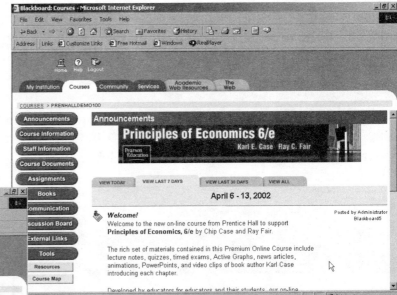

FIGURE A.8
The Announcements Screen. Only navigation buttons in Blackboard 5.

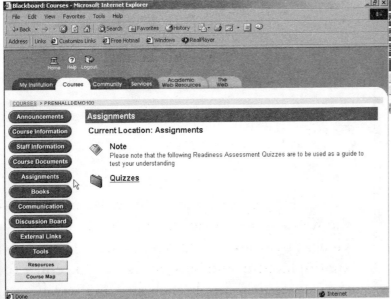

FIGURE A.9 QUIZZES.
You may find quizzes in a folder or as a single link.

QUIZZES

Quizzes may appear under a button like Assignments, or you may see a link to a quiz in the Announcements area.

Quizzes are a little different in Blackboard 5 than in Blackboard 6. In Blackboard 5 all questions will be presented at one time. Here is a step by step approach to taking a quiz in Blackboard 5.

How To Take a Quiz

✔ First, Click the **Take quiz** link or button (Figure A.10). You will be prompted with: Are

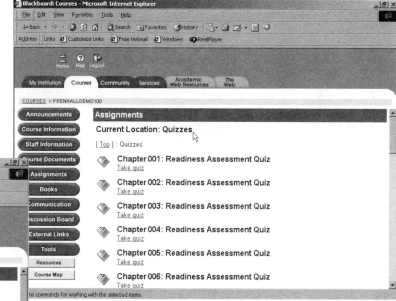

FIGURE A.10 Choosing a Quiz.

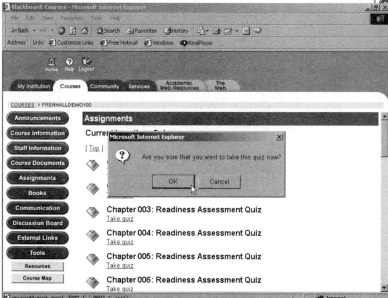

FIGURE A.11 Taking a Quiz.
Click **OK** only if you are ready to take the test. Clicking OK prematurely may block you from taking the quiz.

you sure you want to take this quiz now? (Figure A.11). Be careful. Some tests are set so that you can take them only once. If you click OK, that means you are ready to take the test. If you are not ready and you click OK, you will have to contact your instructor and have that person reset

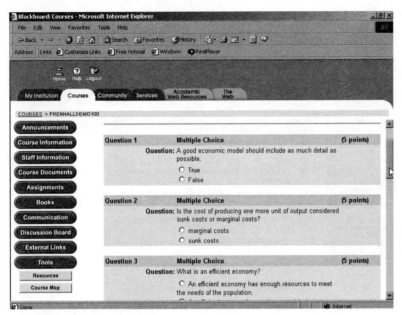

FIGURE A.12 SUBMITTING THE QUIZ.
When taking a quiz be sure to scroll down to see all the questions. Your quiz will not be graded unless you scroll to the bottom and click the **Submit** button.

your test. If you are not ready to take the test, click Cancel, and you can come back to it when you are ready.

✔ Click **OK** if you are ready.

✔ Next, your quiz will be displayed. Look in the Status Bar, and a counter will display if the quiz is timed. Do not surf the Internet in the same browser you are using to take the test. This may break the connection with the server, and you may not be able to submit the test. If you need to look up information while taking a test, open another browser. (To open a new browser in Internet Explorer, go to the browser's file menu and select New→Window. In Netscape, hold down the **Control** key (**Ctrl**) and press the **N** key.)

✔ Once you have completed the test, scroll to the bottom and click the **Submit** button. If you do not click Submit, your results will not be sent to the server and there will be no grade. If you lose your Internet connection while taking a test, your test may not be submitted and you may need to contact your instructor to reset the test. If you have problems, try taking the test again before contacting your instructor.

Communication Tools

Blackboard 5 provides you with three different tools to communicate with faculty and other students. They are

✔ Send E-mail
✔ Discussion Board
✔ Virtual Classroom

In Blackboard 5 Send E-mail and Discussion Board tools are the same. However, in Blackboard 6, Virtual Chat is called Collaboration.

Virtual Classroom/Chat

The Virtual Classroom, or Virtual Chat, is a synchronous discussion. This means that all participants are logged on the system simultaneously.

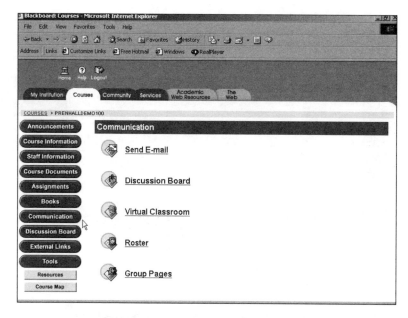

Figure A.13 Communication.
Click the **Communication** button to access Blackboard's communication tools.

Communication is happening live. Users are able to see responses as they are sent.

Location. This text field allows instructors and students to enter URLs to take virtual field trips. When a Web address is added, pressing the **Enter** key on the keyboard submits the request. The Web site is then displayed on the White Board to everyone simultaneously.

White Board. Think of White Board as a drawing tool. If the instructor posts a graphic or links to a Web site, the drawing tool allows chat participants to add comments and draw diagrams.

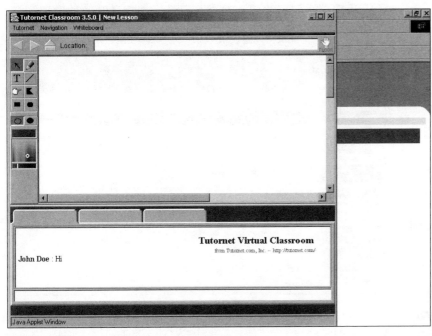

FIGURE A.14 THE BLACKBOARD VIRTUAL CLASSROOM.

Chat Area. Near the bottom of Figure A.14, you will see an area labeled Tutornet Virtual Classroom. This area is the text-based chat component. Beneath this you will see a one-line text box. This text area is where you can write your questions and comments. To submit your questions and comments, press **Enter.** Within seconds, you will see what you wrote in the above text area. In the comment text area, you will see "John Doe: HI." This message will appear on the screens of all users logged into the virtual chat.

Additional Tools

The following Items work the same in Blackboard 5 and 6:

✔ Digital Drop Box
✔ Edit Your Home Page
✔ Personal Information

✔ Calendar

✔ Student Manual

✔ Tasks

✔ Electronic Blackboard

✔ Address Book

Check Grade is a little more limited in Blackboard 5. Blackboard 6 allows instructors to add comments to tests which can be viewed by clicking the grade in the grade book. Blackboard 5's grade book is only a grade reporting mechanism, and students can view only their tests results.

If you need additional information for any of these tools, refer to Module 7: Additional Tools.

FIGURE A.15 TOOLS.
Click the Tools button to access Blackboard's student tools.

Index